Beyond the Dream

Richard Dare

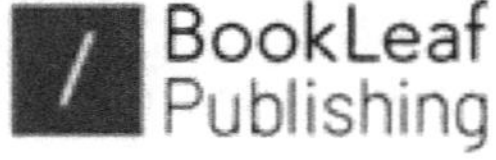

Presentation by *BookLeaf Publishing*

Web: www.bookleafpub.com

E-mail: info@bookleafpub.com

ISBN: 9789357210294

First edition 2022

DEDICATION

To you,

Set the Stage

Insomniac
Raise your spirit
Today we sleep

The open fields of your castle burn
As the horizon learns

A theatre of shadows puts on their play
Once and finally
The sifted limbs of the sunken singer
can be found out back

A knowledge
A place of strength
Hold no punches
and run

A nixed and bloppy substance
Feigns softness, where truly
All things show solid reality
in the land's dream

A Pity upon Persepolis

She's not fire,
She's thunder.
Only a human,
a frail wonder.
She's a finite source
of caring generosity;
A pilot flying
towards freedom.
An arrangement of pieces and particulates that
form perfectly
into You.
You and no other
You who has given hope to all
and to more.

When the heart shines brightest,
it does so because of love.
When the heart shines lightest,
it does so because of fear.
When the heart shines darkest,
it does so because of hate.
Because of hate,
this world shines darkly.
Because of this world,
she shines no more.

Silence

Silence
Is a version of past events that never ceases in repeating itself.
Lesions or liaisons, we bare the cost of silence and hand it to our leaders.
Empathy ever-lacking, they barge at the barricades of our preserved meaning.
Needing a way to unsew these threads and call for help, we cry.
Convenient that, with strewn ambition; my crewmate claws across their face and throat.
Evisceration investigation for silly tongues forever swallowed, and vocal doors slammed shut.

Pieces, Memories and Escapades

If life were to be so memorable
Then how could we forget those arrangements?
Past lives and adventures
Even current life escapades
Eventually evade and elude us
Until there is nothing left, no more memory at
all
Until our thoughts and dreams are no more
Until we see nothing of the past or any previous
life
Even though we believe the answers to be there-
If there's more than just one's judgment
What is there to say about this lack of control?
If solemn wishes and better breathing blooms
there
Then that is where we must go-
but what of the others? The animals and such?
Are they the same as us?
Shall we construe common sense and
constructed science
with what is so clearly false?
Or is it important to believe
that our dear wishes will come true
and that no one is actually gone

But It Won't

5

Serenade my
forever scene
with washing strands of blue.

Entirely surround me
in that dashing way
you bring my bon-fire light.

Whatever could happen to be
could've really mattered to me

Robbed of Red

Fingers tracing
down sanguine stockings
plucking every chord.

For now the mystery
of daemon war wanderers
resolves at the foot the divine,
occult to their lust.

If only true
all wars would find their foil
in the brothel of Bethel.

Leshraq

Hurried by the promise,
desolate soles wanders.

Without light or guiding voice,
she listens to the sound of meaning
and ensures her path home.

But the terrors make their sudden move
and catch her without guard
and make her their meal.

She does not perish, she does not suffer.
She prepares dinner for the demons instead
and invites them to the table of her mind.

Monstrosities no match for the woe that dwells
above.
Their souls are severed from their twisted spirits
and become one-

with her,
Despair.

Words on a Screen

Words, words, words on a screen.
Of all the things I've ever seen…
    this one is for you.
Lay it down, on the fire;
every last
bean,
bread
and pacifier
and let them know
this be true.
They will not be caught
if they tiptoe to the spot.
    Split,
    splat,
    splot out the sun!
and let it be dark.
Every last word, every last one, it is no fun
That's why this is done.
I will be back…
…I will return…
I always have...
I always will…

Invalid Memory

Sorta coulda wished you'd had done it already
Kinda just thought you had.
Little bit like a mystery
A search to find that bad

Without a single memory
Within a flustered thought
You force invalid melody
With electric rock

Forever and ever a platitude
Forever, wherever a hope.
If ever the weather breaks the storm
you'll find all hearts porked.

Frozen

They say
bad things come in threes,
like holding your hand in mine.

Bad things come in threes,
Kissing you lips in time-
for the moment, that you want this
let's stay here, be this.

They say, bad things come in threes,
like how I'm holding on hope for you.

Go on

Though it appears that this path
is sunk, uneven and glossed with grass
These stones, only you can see
a story, only you succeed

FTL

Faster than light
Faster than all

There's only one certain way
to bring the empire's fall

Catch that ship
don't let it get away
The reformation of the galaxy
cannot go astray

No, no-
That's not the play
Damn!
Today is doomsday

Muddied Waters

13

brown and sloshing sideways
swampy persistent liquid
drenches fine attire, all
the culprit smiles with glee
a muddy blue fish of the Okefenokee

The Dreamer

I came into this world inspired by flame
It's the truth
No shame.
It was in the field that I spied
A name, I complied
And wondered it's true meaning.
From dusk to birth
The wheel was set to spin
An object of emotion
And bond to gravity

If life were a game
I'd be end-phase carry
With early support skills
That burn before they heal.
A thought
Lost in mind
Finding the will to survive
In the dark

They raised me
King and Queen
I was Prince
We were seen
We all got confused

When the kingdom of shein
Was knocked out of it's place
And meant to rehabilitate

I never saw him again
The heartbreaking king
Who sold our golden souls
For some other thing
He left his children
To dream without a dream

For the longest time
I was in darkness
But the darkness grayed
The smoked out light
Made friends through might
And when we left the hollow nursery
We saw the signs of sourcery
And stayed loyal to the language.

Those first fine friends
Never looked to me again
And left me to shoulder
The pain of a boulder
And inability to climb any height ahead

It wasn't until now
When I pushed out your styrofoam form
That you started to notice me

And we formed a bond
An act of chemistry
The Scientist, the buff and the sedentary

We joked and we laughed
Until it all came echoing back
Those same loathsome words
Echoing back until we rocked
Back and forth forever and ever
and ever, and ever.

Sifting through books
The rabbit sought the seeker
And wished for him with wholesome words
Until he happened upon to meet her
In their fantasy and in their worlds
They trusted the feelings in their hearts to be real

Animals are Perfect

17

Animals are perfect
Humans are not
Aliens are wise for leaving man on earth
but cruel for not saving the animals

I know somewhere out there
They could make a system of zoos
Where piggies, dodos, and chickadees too
Enjoy serenity without the pollution of you

Princess Charming

Beautiful beyond imagination
Every day a blessing
Loving, a heart of light
Lost, no prince in sight
Adorn her bouquet, a rose

so she'll be remembered always

Under Line

Under Line
Meticulously developed
Endlessly advancing
Technological taxonomies
Warring with warranties

When all the men are packed in the same bowl
It's as if there were
None.
Nobody ever said it would be easy, though
Easy shouldn't be desired.
Real winners never quit
Real winners take what isn't theirs
And repurposes it
Eliminating the prior competition ensures
Victory for oneself.
Ever get that feeling as if you're going to lose
your
Rick's?
Get over it.
I, the tower will raise you high and
Vindicate your heart, body and mind.
Even those dead
the Ultimate opulence
of being alive

will Purge the two words from sight.

Atomic instigation
That stirs the world
Energized revolution and
Meticulous black holes
Stand in our place.

Goddess Reincarnate

I write for you
In memoristic disbelief,
I try to remember.
Every day, another hour
Another sweet, one sour
To let us know what we've become
To let us know where we go.
Such pihpanies of nihilism
Rend all dark.
You know it can't be seen-
The last sun, Merkabah's beam.
Yes
It is rather true.
Ravishing, take me away
If we can't stay.
Let our ideas,
Be.